The Little Monasteries

Frank O'Connor

The Little Monasteries

translations from Irish poetry
mainly of the seventh
to the twelfth centuries

The Dolmen Press

*Set in Pilgrim type with Victor Hammer's
Uncial as titling and printed and published in
the Republic of Ireland at the Dolmen Press,
North Richmond Industrial Estate,
North Richmond Street, Dublin 1.*

Title page drawing by Ruth Brandt.

*First published in an edition limited to
1050 numbered copies, 1963.*

Newly set and printed 1976.

*Distributed in the U.S.A. and in Canada
by Humanities Press Inc., 171 First Avenue,
Atlantic Highlands, N.J. 07716.*

ISBN 0 85105 296 7

© *1963, 1976 Harriet Sheehy.*

Preface

With the exception of 'I Am Stretched on your Grave' (18th c.), 'On the Death of His Wife' (early 13th c.) and two Renaissance poems, Richard Burke's 'Women' and the anonymous 'History of Love', both written about 1600, the poems in this book come from the seventh to the twelfth centuries — the period of the little monasteries which has always fascinated me. Sometimes the language is fantastically difficult. In *Kings, Lords, and Commons* I omitted the third verse from the poem, 'Liadain' because I could wring no sense from it. It was only a few months ago that I learned to read the text correctly. It runs roughly —

>   All my desire
>   Was that we two should keep our tryst
>   And meet in Heaven beyond the fire.

Witness, too 'The Nun of Beare' which I translated first forty years ago from the only available edition, that of Kuno Meyer. In *Kings, Lords, and Commons* I made a number of changes based on the edition of Gerard Murphy in *Early Irish Lyrics*. The present version involves a complete reconstruction, based on my own guesses and the help of some scholar friends, yet even in this I know that certain verses must be misplaced and wrongly translated. As I see it now the poem is really a series of lyrics from a lost eighth-century romance dealing with the Goddess of Munster and St. Cummine. In the romance, the Goddess, regarded as an Irish Mary Magdálen, must have invited Christ to spend the night with her and been converted only on his appearance. I have also revised the translation of the 'Seasons', poems which in Irish are a brilliant pastiche of an archaic Irish metre.

It would be a mere embarrassment to my friends Professors D. A. Binchy and David Greene to list all the improvements that I owe them, and I prefer merely to acknowledge the kindness of both.

Contents

The Seasons	page 9
In the Country	11
The Old Poet	12
The Thirsty Poet	13
The Ex-Poet	14
The Angry Poet	15
Ordeal by Cohabitation	16
Advice to Lovers	17
The Dead Lover	18
On the Death of His Wife	22
Women	25
A History of Love	28
I Am Stretched on Your Grave	30
The Nun of Beare	32
Colum Cille	38
Tears	40
Eve	42
Praise	43
The Protecting Tree	44
The Last Victory	45
Notes	47

The Seasons

Fall is no man's travelling time;
Tasks are heavy; husbandmen
Heed the low light, lingering less.
Lightly their young drop from the deer,
Dandled in the faded fern;
Fiercely the stag stalks from the hill,
Hearing the herd in clamorous call;
Cobbled the mast in windless woods,
Weary the corn upon its canes,
    Colouring the brown earth.
Endless the thorns that foul the fence
Which frames the hollow of some house;
The hard dry ground is filled with fruit,
And by the fort, hard from their height
    Hazelnuts break and fall.

The dark days of the winter world
Waken the tides that boom and break
    The beaches of the earth;
Ill fare the birds of park and plain;
Pleased are the ravens breathing blood
    At black winter's wail.
Winter, sooty dark and damp
The dogs appals who champ and chew,
Upon its chain the stewpot steams
    All the stern dark day.

Spring is icy-crisp and cold,
Keen the draught through every door,
Ducks on the lake lament their lot,
    Loud is the sad crane's cry.
Crafty wolves creep from dark dens,
Drowsy birds wake rustling reeds,
And rouse the beasts they flee before
    Who from the fresh grass spring.

Warm summer is the traveller's time,
The tall trees hush, nor turn nor twist
    At any touch of wind
In woods new laden with their leaves.
And lower still the rivulets run.
    Even the rich grass is warm.

In the Country

A hedge of trees is all around;
   The blackbird's praise I shall not hide;
Above my book so smoothly lined
   The birds are singing far and wide.

In a green cloak of bushy boughs
   The cuckoo pipes his melodies —
Be good to me, God, on Judgment Day! —
   How well I write beneath the trees!

The Old Poet

God be praised who ne'er forgets me
   In my art so high and cold
And still sheds upon my verses
   All the magic of red gold.

The Thirsty Poet

Blessings on King Donal's daughter,
    Gracious Ethna, good indeed,
Who, when I had cased the township
    For rat poison,
Sent me two and thirty wry-necked
    Harnessed hauliers'
  Load of mead.

The Ex-Poet

Once the ex-poet Cuirithir
And I were lovers; there's no cure;
And I am left to bear the pain,
Knowing we shall not meet again.

South of the church there stands a stone
Where the ex-poet sat alone;
I sit there too at close of day
In twilight when I come to pray.

No woman now shall be his mate,
No son nor daughter share his fate,
No thigh beside his thigh repose —
Solitary the ex-poet goes.

The Angry Poet
Clonmacnois, c. 1100

The hound
   Could never be called refined,
So push the tip of his nose
   Up the Master's behind.

The Master
   May amend his scholarly air
If you screw the tip of his nose
   Up in the lackey's rear.

The lackey
   Will have the chance of his life
If you stuff his nose in turn
   In the tail of the Master's wife.

The wife —
   Who is always sniffing around —
May sniff for the rest of her days
   Her nose in the tail of the hound.

Ordeal by Cohabitation

He   So I and my love Liadin
Should sleep together without sin
While any layman on the earth
Would boast of what that chance was worth.

She   Though I and my love Cuirither
Had practised virtue for a year,
Left together for one night
Our thoughts would stray before daylight.

Advice to Lovers

The way to get on with a girl
   Is to drift like a man in a mist,
Happy enough to be caught,
   Happy to be dismissed.

Glad to be out of her way,
   Glad to rejoin her in bed,
Equally grieved or gay
   To learn that she's living or dead.

The Dead Lover

Silence, girl! What can you say?
My thoughts are not of you, they stray;
I think of nothing else tonight
Except the battlefield and fight.

My headless body tossed aside
Lies on the slope whereon I died,
And in that heap my head you see
Near those of men who died with me.

A lovers' tryst is waste of breath
Beside the final tryst with death,
And so the lovers' tryst we made
I can keep only as a shade.

All was foredoomed. Woe for my pride!
My resting place was set aside,
The battle to which I should go
Where a strange hand would strike me low.

I am not the first in body's heat
Who found some outland woman sweet,
And though our parting tryst be drear
It was your love that brought me here.

It was for love alone I came,
Leaving my gentle wife in shame:
Had I but known what would befall
How gladly would I have shunned it all.

My mercenaries, true to the last,
My bright-faced outlaw band held fast,
That lofty yew-wood doomed to fall
Into the earth that covers all.

Had they but lived to swing a sword
Not unavenged had been their lord,
And if their master still had breath
Not unavenged would be their death.

No certain shadow of defeat
Could overcloud their battle heat,
The stock of men who knew no fear
They sang and called, their voices clear.

Up to the moment when they died
They were still active, full of pride;
Fearful the storm through which they passed —
The green wood holds them all at last.

Why should you spend a night of dread
Alone among the unburied dead?
Why linger with an old love there?
Back to your home! But take my gear.

For much that living men held dear
Is all about you here and here,
Valueless to the Great Queen
Who washes entrails in the stream.

From the spear's point that crowned the fight
The Great Queen flashed upon my sight;
Hers are the spoils that please her best;
Well may she laugh at all the rest.

Boldly she tosses back her hair;
Only the brave her eye can dare.
Be calm, there is nothing she can do,
Near as she seems to such as you.

From human things I must take flight
After my men with the first light;
Already the night's end has come;
Do not stay here, back to your home!

Men will remember many a day
The song of Fohad Cananne;
Famous shall be my speech with you
So do what I would have you do.

That future men may hear me praised
Above me let a great tomb be raised;
Your labour shall not be in vain,
Your love being passed, to ease its pain.

Now my pierced body must descend
To torture where the fiends attend;
Worldly love is a foolish thing
Beside the worship of Heaven's king.

It is the blackbird! Once again
He calls at dawn to living men;
My voice, my face are of the dead.
Silence! What is there to be said?

On the Death of His Wife

I parted from my life last night,
   A woman's body sunk in clay:
The tender bosom that I loved
   Wrapped in a sheet they took away.

The heavy blossom that had lit
   The ancient boughs is tossed and blown;
Hers was the burden of delight
   That long had weighed the old tree down.

And I am left alone tonight
   And desolate is the world I see
For lovely was that woman's weight
   That even last night had lain on me.

Weeping I look upon the place
   Where she used to rest her head —
For yesterday her body's length
   Reposed upon you too, my bed.

Yesterday that smiling face
   Upon one side of you was laid
That could match the hazel bloom
   In its dark delicate sweet shade.

Maelva of the shadowy brows
   Was the mead-cask at my side;
Fairest of all flowers that grow
   Was the beauty that has died.

My body's self deserts me now,
   The half of me that was her own,
Since all I knew of brightness died
   Half of me lingers, half is gone.

The face that was like hawthorn bloom
   Was my right foot and my right side;
And my right hand and my right eye
   Were no more mine than hers who died.

Poor is the share of me that's left
   Since half of me died with my wife;
I shudder at the words I speak;
   Dear God, that girl was half my life.

And our first look was her first love;
   No man had fondled ere I came
The little breasts so small and firm
   And the long body like a flame.

For twenty years we shared a home,
   Our converse milder with each year;
Eleven children in its time
   Did that tall stately body bear.

It was the King of hosts and roads
   Who snatched her from me in her prime:
Little she wished to leave alone
   The man she loved before her time.

Now King of churches and of bells,
   Though never raised to pledge a lie
That woman's hand — can it be true? —
   No more beneath my head will lie.

                           Murrough O'Daly, *c.* 1200

Women

Every man in Ireland caught
  By some girl with eyes of blue
Dolefully laments his lot
  Unless her hair be golden too.

What has this to do with me?
  No fanaticism I share
For blue or black in someone's eye
  Or the colour of her hair.

Golden mane or rosy grace
  Can never be my whole delight.
Dusky be the woman's face
  And her hair as black as night.

Black was the dam of her who brought
  Troy into the dust of old,
And the girl for whom they fought,
  Helen, was all white and gold.

Beautiful surely were the two
  Though one was dark and one was fair.
No one who ever saw them knew
  Which was the lovelier of the pair.

In little shells it may befall
  The loveliest of pearls is found,
And God created three things small —
  The horse, the woman and the hound.

Public confession suits my case,
  And all may hear what I would say —
In women, such is my disgrace,
  I never found a thing astray.

Though some are small I like them neat
  And some are tall of them I sing;
Two long legs to grace the sheet
  Are satisfaction for a king.

Foam may be brighter than her skin
  Or snow upon the mountain cold,
I'll take what pack I find her in
  And think her sweeter for being old.

Nor should I slight a relative
  For someone from outside the state;
Though novelty keep love alive
  Kinsmen love at double rate.

Nor do I ask for intellect:
  A little scholarship will pass;
All that of women I expect
  Is to know water-cress from grass.

I don't require them cold or warm;
  Widows have knowledge and good sense
But there is still a certain charm
  In a young girl's inexperience.

I like them in church, demure and slow,
   Solemn without, relaxed at home;
I like them full of push and go
   When love has left me overcome.

I find no fault in them, by God,
   But being old and gone to waste
Who still are girls at forty odd —
   And every man may suit his taste.

Richard Burke

A History of Love

This is Love's history
    And how it all began:
As an authority
    I am your foremost man.

Diarmuid the bold and gay,
    Chief of the warrior bands,
With Grania one day
    Invented holding hands.

While Ulster's Hound as well,
    When a Greek girl went by,
Falling beneath her spell,
    Was first with the glad eye.

Naisi, home from the chase,
    Weary, inspired with bliss,
Seeing Deirdre don her trews,
    Endowed us with the kiss.

The son of Conall met
    Their challenges with grace
And left us in his debt
    By figuring the long embrace.

Avartach, king of the fairies,
    Following in their track,
With his arbutus berries
    Put a girl upon her back.

Ceadach, master of trades,
   Seeing them still unversed —
Those white-skinned Irish maids —
   Made women of them first.

And Angus as they say —
   Lord of the Sacred Hill —
First took their clothes away,
   And gave them perfect skill.

Learning that hearts can break
   Under Love's miseries
Beside a Munster lake
   Glas filled the air with sighs.

Lamenting to soft strings
   And moans upon the pipe
Were Mongan's offerings
   To woo some timid wife.

But I, to my own grief,
   First opened Jealousy's door —
This is my tale in brief —
   And now it shuts no more.

I Am Stretched on Your Grave

I am stretched on your grave
    And would lie there forever;
If your hands were in mine
    I'd be sure we'd not sever.
My apple tree, my brightness,
    'Tis time we were together
For I smell of the earth
    And am stained by the weather.

When my family thinks
    That I'm safe in my bed
From night until morning
    I am stretched at your head,
Calling out to the air
    With tears hot and wild
My grief for the girl
    That I loved as a child.

Do you remember
    The night we were lost
In the shade of the blackthorn
    And the chill of the frost?
Thanks be to Jesus
    We did what was right,
And your maidenhead still
    Is your pillar of light.

The priests and the friars
   Approach me in dread
Because I still love you
   My love and you dead,
And would still be your shelter
   From rain and from storm,
And with you in the cold grave
   I cannot sleep warm.

The Nun of Beare

I

Wealth is all you ask today;
    Women do not touch your heart;
But when I was young and gay
    Men and women played their part.

Well beloved were the men
    Who to you their place have lost;
Though they gave so much to love
    Of their gifts they did not boast.

While today you ask for all
    And get little in return,
And in boastfulness recall
    The small gifts that love would spurn.

II

I, the old woman of Beare,
    Who wore dresses ever-new
Have so lost the shape I wore
    Even an old one will not do.

And my hands as you can see
    Are but bony wasted things,
Hands that once would grasp the hand
    Clasp the royal neck of kings.

Oh, my hands as you have seen
Are so bony and so thin
That a boy might start in dread
Feeling them about his head.

My right eye has lost its light,
   Auctioned with my lost estate,
And the other too has gone —
   Bankruptcy must be my fate.

Ale is poured but not for me,
   For my wedding no sheep dies;
Since my hair is all but grey
   This poor veil is no surprise.

Though I care
Nothing for what binds my hair,
   I had headgear bright enough
When the kings for love went bare.

Long ago the foaming steed
And the chariot with its speed
Were the gifts the kings bestowed —
May they get as much from God!

I who had my day with kings
   And drank deep of mead and wine
Drink whey-water with old hags
   Sitting in their rags and pine.

Cummine

May my cups be cups of whey,
May thy will be done, I pray,
And the prayer, O living God
Quells the madness in my blood.

Nun

But I must rage
Who wear the shaggy cloak of age,
My body stuck with threads of grey
Like an old tree that rots away.

Cummine

Yet my King throws a different cloak
   In springtime over hill and glen,
The heavenly fuller who can tread
   The earth till all is smooth again.

Nun

I scorn all aged things but one,
   Femuin and its shining plain;
While I wither here alone
   Femuin's ways are gold again.

Femuin, Bregon, sacring stone,
Sacring stone and Ronan's Throne,
   Storms have sacked them but their cheeks
Are not withered like my own.

Girls are gay
When the year draws on to May,
   But for me, so poor am I,
Sun will never light the day.

Summer sun and autumn sun
These I knew and they are gone,
And the winter time of men
Comes and they come not again.

Madly did I spend my prime —
   What is there to cause me rage? —
If in prayer I had passed the time
   Should I not wear the cloak of age?

Cummine

Where are they? Ah, well you know
To and fro they row and row;
Like the reeds on Alma's Ford
They sleep cold who slept not so.

Nun

'Tis many a day
Since I sailed upon youth's bay;
   Year on year has scored my flesh
Since my fresh sweet strength went grey.

Many a day
I have been as cold as they:
   Even in the sun I wear my shawl;
Age has put me too away.

My body bows as though alone
It sought to give the earth its own;
   Let God's Son when he deems it due
Come to me to recall his loan.

Why should God's Son not come my way
   And spend the night beneath my roof?
Whoever else I turned away
   When did I hold a man aloof?

I too am cold, but let it be!
   All great beauties know despair;
The glittering ones they sleep with pass
   And leave them to the dark and prayer.

III

Ebbtide is all my grief;
   Bitter age has sucked my blood;
But though I get no relief
   Merrily returns its flood.

Happy island of the main
To you the tide returns again,
But to me it comes no more
Over the blank deserted shore.

Floodtide!
   Flood or ebb upon the strand,
What the floodtide brings to you
   Ebbtide carries from my hand.

Floodtide!
   And the ebb with hurrying fall;
I have seen many, ebb and flow,
   Ay, and now I know them all.

Floodtide
   Cannot reach me where I call;
None in darkness seeks my side;
   Cold the hand that lies on all.

Seeing, I can scarcely say
— 'This is such a place'; today
What was water far and wide
Changes with the ebbing tide.

IV

Woe to all
   Those who perish in their pride!
Who have scarcely seen their flood
   Ere they see their ebbing tide.

My flood
   Spared the gift that might have died
Until Jesus bought it back
   When I was weary at ebbtide.

Colum Cille

Would to God, O Son of Mary,
  Sailing, rowing,
I could cross the sea to Ireland,
  Homeward going!

Up Lough Foyle, beneath Benvenagh
  Into Derry,
Where at evening the swan's call would
  Make me merry.

Were my ship but anchored, flouting
  The waves' beating,
All the seagulls would come shouting
  Their shrill greeting.

Happy is the son of Deema
  In his dwelling;
He can hear there, west from Durrow,
  Music swelling.

Hear the murmur of the elmtree
  Branches sighing,
And the clapping wings of startled
  Blackbirds crying.

Stags about Ros Grencha belling
  From some clearing,
And the cuckoo in the woods at
  Summer's nearing.

Would to God I had fled the battle
   Nor been banished!
There the three things I most cherished
   Ever vanished.

Three things dearest under Heaven
   To my sorrow
I have forfeited, Teerleedy,
   Derry, Durrow.

Tears

Grant me, gracious God,
   To allay my fears
While I walk this world,
   Wave on wave of tears.

A vessel full of tears
   Give me for my own
That my perilous path
   I may tread alone.

Gentle Christ, my grief
   That my cheeks do not flow
With the floods you gave
   To Magdalen long ago!

My grief that from my breast
   Reaching every part
Pours no waterfall
   To freshen limbs and heart!

For each wise old man
   Who sought pain and loss
In your kingdom's quest,
   For your shameful cross —

For all sinners here
   Who their tears renew,
My sins, O my God,
   Let me weep them too.

For your goodness' sake,
　For your kingly state,
Grant me a well of tears
　Ere it be too late.

Let my heart drip tears
　As your heart dripped blood —
Who can give me tears
　Only you, my God?

Eve

I am the wife of Adam, Eve;
   For my transgression Jesus died;
I stole Heaven from those I leave;
   'Tis me they should have crucified.

Dreadful was the choice I made,
   I who was once a mighty queen;
Dreadful, too, the price I paid —
   Woe, my hand is still unclean!

I plucked the apple from the spray
   Because of greed I could not rule;
Even until their final day
   Women still will play the fool.

Ice would not be anywhere,
   Wild white winter would not be;
There would be no hell, no fear
   And no sorrow but for me.

Praise

Raise your voice in praise, O people!
    Praise the Lord God everywhere
Since the little birds must praise Him —
    They who have no soul but air.

The Protecting Tree
A.D. 621

The thunderous shining waves have spanned
   The ocean and the solid land,
And Conaing too, for all his skill,
Swamped in his wicker coracle.

At Conaing in his little boat
   The woman throws her hair of foam,
And then she turns away to gloat
   Upon the tree that guards his home.

The Last Victory
Maelshechnaill II, 1022

Thirty swift days
   To the end of his story
From that night at Athboy
   And his final red glory.

Notes

THE EX-POET and ORDEAL BY COHABITATION. Both from 'Liadain and Cuirithir'. St. Cummine, as author of a famous Penitential, was regarded by Irish storytellers as a proper man to handle lovers — see 'The Nun of Beare'. He tests the progress in virtue of the two poet-lovers by making them sleep together with a young student between them. The experiment is a failure and Cuirithir departs in anger. 'Ex-poet', as well as having its ordinary meaning, is also a bitter play on the Old Irish word for 'monk', which might be rendered 'ex-laic'.

THE ANGRY POET. Supposed to be spoken by Feidlimid, a scholarly king-bishop of Munster in the 9th century who plundered Clonmacnois — according to Munster storytellers — in revenge for the treatment he received when he went there as a poor scholar. More probably the authentic utterance of a real poor scholar.

THE DEAD LOVER. From a ninth-century historical poem of fifty verses. Fohad, who is leader of a *fian* or *amusrad* — a band of mercenaries — elopes with the wife of another mercenary chief. He is killed in battle but returns to keep his tryst. Such historical poems are usually very dull, being full of unnecessary information, but the language of this poem is of extraordinary beauty.

COLUM CILLE. An 11th century poem about a 6th century saint who is supposed to have exiled himself in Iona for his part in the battle of Cuil Dremne, A.D. 561.

THE PROTECTING TREE. On the drowning of Conaing in the Irish Sea. The tree which the sea-wife mocks is the tree of Tortu, the sacred tree of Conaing's family. The form — that of the double epigram in contrasting metres—is, so far as I know, peculiar to Irish literature.